Our Story, By Us, For Us!
The Story of British People of African Caribbean Origin

First published in paperback in 2013 by Reach Society Publishing

British Library Cataloguing in Publication Data

ISBN: 978-0-9575624-0-0

Printed and bound in Great Britain by Print Express, Ruislip, London

Cover designed by Print Express, Ruislip, London

Reach Society Publishing
A division of RSCL Ltd, trading as Reach Society
C/o Collards, 2 High Street, Kingston-Upon-Thames, Surrey, KT1 5EY

Website: www.reachsociety.com

Dedication

This book is dedicated to British people of African Caribbean origin.

Contents

Acknowledgements

The authors wish to thank the team of young adults Koral, Ellen, Dave, Leon and Ritchie for their many comments during the preparation of this publication. We also wish to thank Paul Butler, managing director, Butler & Trinity Ltd; Dr Robert Berkeley, director, Runnymede Trust; Diane Edwards and Elizabeth Mullings-Smith, trustees, British Foundation for University of the West Indies for their interest; Robin Walker, author and black studies expert, for reminding us of the importance and value of cultural esteem; and Lord Herman Ouseley, patron of Reach Society, for his generous support.

The history project team would be happy to hear from readers who wish to share the contributions of their family members and friends to the African Caribbean story.

You can contact us on: **historyproject@reachsociety.com**

Foreword

In composing the "ROOTS OF THE FUTURE" Project, launched by the Prince of Wales for the Commission for Racial Equality (CRE) back in the mid 1990s, the main questions I posed for Britain's diverse multicultural society in understanding the contributions made over centuries by the Black and Minority Ethnic people to British economic development were:

Who am I? Who are you? Who are we?

For me, and for many Black British people living in Britain, knowing who you are, understanding the history of the struggles for equality, fair treatment and human rights and knowing about the positive contributions of Black people to Britain's development over the centuries, are critical and essential characteristics. This will enable us to have the feelings of "belonging", which are hard to have when faced with discrimination, abuse and exclusion.

Fortunately, in contemporary Britain, we have the development of new emergent organisations, such as the Reach Society. These organisations will help to stimulate positive learning about ourselves and other people in our world so that we can make our individual and collective contributions to the society and country of which we are a part.

The British people of African Caribbean origin are a distinct component of today's Black British population. Their story is important and unique; and this publication confirms how our society has been strengthened and enriched by their energy, creativity and diverse contributions.

For me, and indeed for all of us, it is important to be informed, be proud, be confident, be positive and be responsible; for these are the building blocks for us to be our best!

Lord Herman Ouseley, Kt

Preface

The supply of relevant, meaningful and inclusive information about the experiences and contributions of British people of African Caribbean background is patchy. The gap in the supply of meaningful and useful information about this community has left most of its people with a chronic knowledge gap.

For the last 65 years or so British people of African Caribbean background have lived in the UK without having enough information about the contributions and achievements of people from their cultural background; and the little they have gleaned, mostly from the media, relates mainly to crime, under-achievement and entertainment, to the exclusion of most other aspects of their lives.

Lack of awareness on this level is deeply concerning and should not be tolerated by the community. Consequently, this condition needs to be corrected so that the community will quickly develop an accurate sense of its worth, contributions and usefulness to itself, and to the wider UK community. In so doing the level of esteem within the African Caribbean community in Britain is expected to change for the better.

Reach Society has chosen to undertake the task of closing this knowledge gap, to raise the awareness of young British people of African Caribbean origin, and their community. They will learn about the journey of their ancestors and their families to develop their potential and growth; and to define their destiny driven by faith, desire, ambition, hard work to establish a better life for their families. The Society sees this publication as the beginning of a process for strengthening the community's knowledge and understanding of its journey.

Dr Dwain A. Neil
Chairman, Reach Society

Chapter 1

Who do you think you are?

Who am I? This is a question that everyone asks at some point in his or her life. For every one of us English speakers of African Caribbean background living in the UK, the answer is as given below.

We are coming from the same people who gave the UK Val McCalla (founder of The Voice newspaper, 1982); Tony Wade (entrepreneur and director of Dyke and Dryden); Leroy Reid (founder of Leroy Reid and Co, accountancy firm); Dr Harold Moody (medical doctor and founder of the League of Coloured People, 1931); and Dr Alison Wint (medical doctor & daughter of Dr Arthur Wint, Olympic 400m gold medallist 1948 – the first by an African Caribbean person).

We are coming from the same people who gave the UK Lord Bill Morris (former leader of the Transport & General Worker's Union from 1991); Lord Herman Ouseley (former chairman of the Commission for Racial Equality); Linford Christie (sprinter and 100m Olympic champion); Jessica Ennis (2012 heptathlon Olympic champion); Diane Abbott (first African Caribbean female MP in the British Parliament); Dame Jocelyn Barrow (educator and community champion for social change); Baroness Valerie Amos (erstwhile chair, Equal Opportunities Commission and Labour Party minister) and David Lammy, MP.

We are coming from the same people who gave the UK Colin Jackson (world record 110m hurdler); Adrian Lester (lead actor in the popular TV serial Hustle); Naomie Harris (actress in Skyfall, the 2012 James Bond movie); Juliette Foster, Moira Stewart & Sir Trevor McDonald (news presenters on the BBC, Sky Broadcasting and ITV); Jazzy B and Courtney Pine (pioneering musicians & performers); Zadie Smith and Andrea Levy (prize winning authors); Garth Crooks, John Barnes and Theo Walcott (premier league footballers, and John and Garth became sports pundits and commentators); Louis Smith (Gymnast, 2012 Olympic silver medallist); Dr Keith Davidson (headteacher, director of education and author); Dr Donald Palmer (scientist and senior lecturer, Royal Veterinary College, University of London) and Robin Walker (teacher, historian, author and black studies expert) – to name but a small number(see their images in the photo gallery).

So who are these people, these English speakers of African Caribbean background? Where did they come from and what brought them to the UK? To answer these questions, and the many others that flow from them, we have chosen to write their story, and in so doing write our story.

The story of these people began in the early 1600s when Britain took control of a tiny uninhabited island we have come to know as Barbados. Then over the next several decades it took control of several more islands in the Caribbean Sea. The records show that Britain was seeking a share of the Caribbean region in order to get land from which it could generate wealth, in much the same way as other European nations were doing such as Portugal, Spain, France and The Netherlands.

Records reveal that Britain took control of Barbados in 1625, which was uninhabited. Britain then used it as a base from which to acquire other islands and countries in the region such as Saint Kitts & Nevis (1628), Montserrat (Irish folks in 1631), Antigua & Barbuda (1632), The Bahamas (1647), Anguilla (1650), Jamaica (1655), The Cayman Islands (1670), British Virgin Islands (1672), Turks & Caicos Islands (1754), Grenada (1762), Dominica (1763), Saint Vincent & The Grenadines (1763), Tobago (1763),Trinidad (1797), Saint Lucia (1803), Guyana (1831) and Belize (1862). The last two are countries in South & Central America. Collectively they make up the islands and countries that came under the control of the British Crown.

In pursuit of wealth creation, Britain cultivated different crops in these territories in the Caribbean region. However, in order to cultivate the lucrative sugar cane a large number of workers were required. To meet this demand for manpower, Britain arranged for the purchase and the abduction of people from the countries on the west coast of the African continent.

Records reveal that Britain, in common with other European nations, generated great wealth from the cultivation of crops in the Caribbean region, using hundreds of thousands of African people. It suited their purposes to regard African people as property. Consequently, African people were bought and sold for profit and forced to work extraordinarily long hours on plantations in the Caribbean region that were owned and controlled by British people.

Put simply, all Africans acquired in this way were over-worked so that large numbers died within a few years. During their short lives they were abused physically, emotionally and psychologically. Furthermore, the children born to these Africans did not escape this inhumane treatment. They too were forced into a life of on going abuse as soon as they were old enough. So from the 1620s to 1834, several millions of these Africans and their descendants were forced to endure over-work and every kind of abuse imaginable. This period we will refer to as the wilderness years in the story of the English speakers of African Caribbean background.

Chapter 2

The Wilderness Years
(1620s to 1834, roughly 214 years, or 8.5 generations)

Records tell us that the wilderness years lasted for roughly two hundred years, from 1620s to 1834, and affected several million people of African origin. This period of bleak existence for around eight generations of Africans came to an end in 1834 when the British Parliament passed the Emancipation Act in 1833. It outlawed the practice of holding people of African descent against their will, in order to over-work them for no pay or reward. It became common practice to inflict extreme punishment on them whenever they refused to comply with the wishes of their owners, or tried to escape from their abusers; this situation is commonly known as enslavement.

The 1833 Act was implemented in 1834 and it required the newly freed people to stay on plantations for six years as apprentices in conditions that should have been marginally improved. The Apprenticeship component of the 1833 Act was enacted for just four of the designated six years, ending in1838, because of the continued abuse of apprentices by plantation owners and their enforcers.

Despite the brutality and humiliation of their situation, these abused African people never gave up hope; and there were several episodes of organised resistance, and attempts to escape this systematic abuse; such as listed below:

In Jamaica captive Africans resisted the British in the First Maroon War (1654 to1739) and kept their freedom and land; and in the 1760s, there was Tacky's rebellion or uprising. In Grenada captive Africans fought in the 1790s, this is recorded as Fedon's Revolution; and in Barbados captive Africans fought for their freedom in 1816, this is recorded as the Bussa Rebellion.

In Guyana captive Africans fought for freedom in 1763, this is recorded as the Berbice Uprising in which half of the whites on plantations in the country were killed before it was ended. In Jamaica captive Africans resisted in 1831, this is recorded as the Sam Sharpe Rebellion. In several of the smaller islands in the Caribbean region there were many acts of resistance from captive Africans, which were put down with brutality by plantation owners, but this did not remove the Africans' desire to fight for their liberty.

What were the implications for Africans transported against their will to islands in the Caribbean region and countries in the Americas? They were permanently separated from their local communities; friends and family members. They were separated and sent to islands and countries hundreds of miles apart, never to be reunited.

They were forced to interact and live with people from other African countries they had little knowledge about, and no understanding of their languages or cultural practices. Their dignity and feelings were disregarded and they were left vulnerable to abuse from anyone, be they other people held as property, or British plantation owners and their hired enforcers who could do as they pleased with them, without fear of any consequences.

Faced with these conditions many Africans chose to end their lives, but others chose to hold on to life. For them to endure their bleak emotional wilderness they had to reassess their attitude to life, and adopt tactics that would help to keep them alive.

To cope with their captivity and to survive their bleak existence they had to change. The Africans from diverse backgrounds and their descendants (born in the Caribbean region) were able to survive by doing several things. They learnt to put aside their tribal differences that were important in their former homelands. They learnt to form new friendships with other people from different African countries and cultural backgrounds. They constructed new languages to communicate with each other, and they learnt the language of their abusers, English. They also kept hope alive by learning the stories of other oppressed people from the Christian Bible; and they prayed for deliverance from the wilderness years, from captivity and the inhumane abuse.

The vast majority of the Africans held in captivity were not literate, as they were never taught to read. Nevertheless, a very small number secretly learnt how to read with the help of some missionaries and faith leaders who did not support the inhumane treatment of the Africans and their offspring born in the Caribbean region.

The wilderness years came to an end not because the plantation owners had a change of heart. It came to an end because of the effort of people in Britain who campaigned for reform; people in the abolition of slavery movement that included Quakers, freed Africans such as Olaudah Aquiano, and politicians like William Wilberforce, MP. They were essential to the passing of legislation in 1807 that ended the transportation of people newly kidnapped from Africa. They were also important to the passing of the additional legislation in 1833 that ended the system of holding Africans and their descendants as captive unpaid labourers, which was implemented in 1834.

The introduction of this legislation heralded the start of a new stage in the lives of the people, Africans brought to and the ones born in the Caribbean region, we now refer to as African Caribbean people. This new stage in their lives would be known as the age of growth and development.

Chapter 3

The age of growth and development
(1834 to 1948, roughly 114 years, or 4.5 generations)

From the decree in 1834 to end enslavement and begin the short lived system of apprenticeship, the English speakers of African Caribbean origin were faced with a number of serious issues and challenges. How they responded to them would determine their survival and their rate of development in the Caribbean region.

Emancipation found African Caribbean people scattered across a number of islands in the Caribbean region and a few countries in Central and South America. The vast majority owned no land, so they had no place to grow the crops that would provide the food needed for basic survival. They also had virtually no money to purchase the things needed. They were people who were never taught to read, so information was transmitted mainly by word of mouth from person to person.

In addition, they were faced with the huge challenge of how to break their dependency on their plantation abusers for their basic needs; because without any means of their own, without any social or political voice (they had no right to vote) their outlook was bleak.

The new system of apprenticeship stipulated in the 1833 Emancipation Act introduced some changes such as reduced working hours, minimal wages, and other basic rights; but plantation owners made sure that their former slaves, who they saw as just objects or property, were no better off under this new system. Indeed freed African Caribbean people quickly fell into severe debt to the plantation owners, as this was not a relationship of equals. In short, the plantation abusers continued their inhumane practices and behaviours towards African Caribbean people. .

The African Caribbean living in Trinidad, Dr. Jean Baptiste Phillipe, wrote a book, "A Free Mulatto" (1824) which reportedly influenced the decision to end the apprenticeship scheme, after just four years, instead of the planned six years.

The chief source of help that was available to these African Caribbean people were the local missionaries and faith groups who showed a measure of compassion and offered assistance. Many helped these African Caribbean people to move away from the plantations to make fresh starts in many new towns on land acquired by the faith groups.

For all practical purposes, these African Caribbean people were now at the start of a new journey to develop their capabilities, their resources, their social and political voice, their ethnic esteem, and their direction, as they strove to define their destiny as free people. This was after more than two hundred years in which they were deprived of any control over their lives or their destiny.

Over the next hundred years or so, from 1834 to 1948, the records show that these people rose to the challenge. They took extraordinary risks, made enormous sacrifices, worked extremely hard and in so doing made huge strides in their battles against the power of the plantation and merchant classes in their scattered homes, the many islands and countries in Central and South Americas. Below are some of the areas of their growth and development.

Free villages, 1830s to 1840s

New villages were founded by African Caribbean people, with the help of faith groups, away from the plantations. Some free villages established in Jamaica included Oracabessa, Sligoville, Granville, Kettering, Maidstone and Sandy Bay. Through these free villages African Caribbean people were able to purchase their own lots of land or small holdings of around 10 acres for their own use, growing crops for their own consumption and for sale at local markets; and for building homes of their own for their families to live in. The growth of free villages immediately after the emancipation was understandably dramatic, as the newly freed people took control of their lives and started to shape their destiny.

In Jamaica African Caribbean freeholders of land increased from roughly 2,000 in 1838 to almost 8,000 in 1840; and more than 50,000 in 1859. In Barbados, where land was in short supply, African Caribbean freeholders increased from roughly 1,100 in 1844 to around 3,500 in 1859. In St. Vincent, about 8,200 persons built their own homes between 1838 and 1857. In Antigua 67 free villages were founded between 1833 and 1858.

Reading and writing

Faith groups also helped African Caribbean people to learn how to read, write and use numbers which paved the way for many to become church deacons and teachers. Over time others trained to become lawyers, doctors and other professionals increasing their options for employment and wealth generation.

Education

Acquiring literacy skills was important for African Caribbean people as it provided other opportunities for work other than employment on plantations. It also gave them access to information about developments in other parts of the Caribbean and the world at large.

The main providers of public education in the nineteenth and early twentieth centuries came from the faith and charitable organisations. Indeed, these education providers were active long before local governments in the Caribbean region introduced a system of free public primary education and limited secondary education; together with an organised system of teacher training and development.

The Lady Mico Charity, registered in the UK, was an early educational provider that funded the creation of hundreds of elementary schools for African Caribbean children and for training African Caribbean adults to become teachers in the Caribbean region. It has been one of the longstanding charities that underpinned educational development of African Caribbean people from 1835 to the present day.

Strikes 1834 to 1870s

Strike action by freed workers in Jamaica, Trinidad, Guyana and elsewhere had adverse impacts on the survival of a significant number of plantations in these countries. Also hurricanes and the collapse of the price of sugar challenged the viability of sugar plantations in many islands; and as a result a large number of them failed.

1840s traders and crafts people

In the 10 years after emancipation there was a rapid increase in African Caribbean traders and crafts people. Records show that by the 1840s there were roughly 18,000 traders in Jamaica, 12,000 in Barbados, 6,000 in Guyana, and 2,500 in Antigua. Trading provided another source of income, for some African Caribbean people, which was different from working on plantations.

1865 campaigns for social justice

An African Caribbean man of action, Paul Bogle, a deacon at Stony Gut Baptist Church, campaigned for improved social justice for poor African Caribbean people in Jamaica. For this he was hanged as was his fellow Baptist and friend George W. Gordon, an African Caribbean landowner and politician. Overall around 500 African Caribbean people were rounded up and hanged for their support of this campaign. These acts of brutality triggered the transfer of political control from the local white plantation class to Britain, making Jamaica a Crown Colony from 1865. This meant it was no longer ruled by the local white elite.

Marcus Garvey's inspiration, 1914 to 1940

Marcus Garvey was a man of action for social change. He was inspired by the autobiography of Booker T. Washington (a famous African American educator) entitled, "Up from slavery". Garvey travelled widely in America and Europe and became convinced that people of African descent needed to pro-actively define their destiny by generating their own wealth and taking responsibility for their own needs.

With his future wife Amy Ashwood he founded UNIA (Universal Negro Improvement Association) in 1914 in Jamaica. The UNIA motto was "One God, one aim, one destiny!" He was convinced that responsibility for self and own affairs through economic, political and cultural successes was the future for people of African descent everywhere.

His UNIA movement was larger than the Civil Rights movement in the USA in the 1960s; and it inspired thousands of people of African origin to reassess or re-evaluate their perception of themselves. It encouraged thousands of African Caribbean people to take action in order to bring about changes to their social, political and economic conditions in the Caribbean region and North America. It was a huge source of cultural esteem and pride.

Trade union impact

In the decades after Marcus Garvey's UNIA movement men and women of action for social change in Guyana, Jamaica, Trinidad and elsewhere started trade unions to campaign for improved working conditions and terms of employment. In Jamaica they included Norman Manley & Bustamante (who started trade unions). In Trinidad Henry S. Williams founded the Pan African Association. In Jamaica Robert Love established the People's Convention around women's rights, education, adult suffrage and other social issues.

Political parties

Men and women of action for social change worked to win the battles for civil rights and the right to vote. In Dominica it included George Charles Falconer, and in Jamaica it involved Norman Manley and Alexander Bustamante. The African Caribbean region timelines (in the appendices) show some significant achievements such as getting voting rights for African Caribbean people in the islands from the 1940s (over twenty years after it was granted to women in Britain); and getting independence from Britain in the 1960s.

Middle class

African Caribbean people never stopped developing their capabilities. They encouraged, nurtured and supported their children to become experts and professionals in many areas such as teaching, business traders, lawyers, doctors, armed service men and women and other disciplines, and in so doing they created a middle class of people with the capabilities to look ahead and strategise for a better future, in their many island homes across the Caribbean region.

Enterprise class

The more entrepreneurial or business minded of the African Caribbean people supplemented their income from the sale of farm produce, and with income generated from working overseas away from their island homes. Jobs were found in construction in Panama, on farms in North America, Cuba and elsewhere. In the 40 years between 1880 and 1920 records show that roughly 150,000 African Caribbean people travelled to Central and North America to take up jobs.

Defending the "mother country"

During both World Wars 1 & 2 young men and women of African Caribbean origin volunteered to serve in the British armed services, the Army and the Royal Air Force (RAF), for the defence of Britain against its enemies in Europe and elsewhere. Many paid the ultimate sacrifice and lost their lives, and a large number served with distinction and received many commendations.

It is worth noting that in this era the prevailing view in Britain was that their service personnel had to be white men and women only. However, when faced with the extreme conditions of the World Wars Britain eventually accepted African Caribbean men and women who volunteered to defend the "mother country." Records show that a number of the

British Colonies in the Caribbean region gave money and local products to Britain towards the war effort. Furthermore, some islands maintained prisoner of war camps where German enemy sailors were held captive.

Post World War 2 and the Windrush generation

The extreme devastation suffered by Britain at the hands of Nazi Germany in World War 2 (WW2) left Britain short of sufficient British manpower for the rebuilding of the country, or to keep the core infrastructure services working efficiently. African Caribbean men and women who defended Britain in Europe returned to their island homes where they found unemployment and an uncertain future. However, when the second call came from Britain, three years after WW2 in 1948, seeking workers, ex service men and women, and people with the drive and ambition for self development rose to the call. They interpreted the call as an opportunity for work and self improvement.

The first significant group of 492 people who responded to the second call from Britain, the "mother country", came from many parts of the Caribbean region – Jamaica, Trinidad, Guyana, Belize and elsewhere. They paid their fare to travel on the Empire Windrush and arrived in England in June 1948. This was the beginning of the movement of significant numbers of African Caribbean people to Britain over the next 20 years. These migrants shall be known as the Windrush generation.

The University of the West Indies (UWI)

UWI was founded in 1948 and started life as the University College of the West Indies (UCWI). Its function was to provide access to higher education locally in the British Caribbean region. At that time the UCWI was affiliated with the University of London.

From the University's inception, students and faculties have been recognised in fields ranging from the arts and sciences, to business, politics, and sports. African Caribbean people have made extensive use of UWI to develop their academic and professional capabilities over many decades. It has produced many world class alumni such as Nobel Laureates, Rhodes Scholars and Heads of Government.

Chapter 4

The age of new opportunities and new challenges
(1948 to 2013, roughly 65 years, or 2.5 generations)

Records show that Britain was on the winning side when the World War 2 (WW2) ended in 1945. This was achieved with the help of many international allies. African Caribbean people from the Caribbean region were part of the coalition of allies.

People of African Caribbean origins had responded to the call from Britain for volunteers, as it faced the monumental threat of Nazi Germany. Tens of thousands of young men and women of African Caribbean origin, living in the Caribbean region, had been trained to bear arms in defence of Britain, the "mother country". There can be no doubt that people from the Caribbean region played their part in the effort to resist the tyranny of Nazi Germany and its hateful ideology.

After WW2 it soon became clear to Britain that the effort to retain its way of life came at a high price. It now did not have the manpower to undertake the twin peace time challenges of rebuilding its damaged cities and maintaining the vital services such as transportation and health service. So once again Britain turned to its territories in the Caribbean region, once again it called on the English speakers of African Caribbean origin. Once again it called on the young men and women who were minded to see this additional call as an opportunity. Many were willing to take the risk of working overseas in order to help Britain recover from the destructive impact of WW2; and also use the opportunity to develop themselves.

This was the background that led to the employment of large numbers of African Caribbean people in Britain. They were engaged in the National Health Service (NHS) as nurses and doctors, on London Transport buses and trains, in the postal service, in the construction sector rebuilding homes and offices, in the RAF after WW2, in the printing industry, in the clothes making industry and in many other industrial sectors.

The first cohort of 492 young people from the Caribbean region (referred to in last chapter) travelled on the Empire to arrive in 1948 at Tilbury docks, England. These African Caribbean travellers shall be remembered as the Windrush Pioneers.

Roughly a third of the Windrush Pioneers were ex-service men and women who had served in Britain during WW2, so they had some knowledge of life in Britain. However, the majority did not, and for them this was a new adventure that would present both challenges and opportunities. Everyone would be required to adapt in order to survive and succeed.

The real stories of those who travelled to the UK either on the Empire Windrush or subsequent voyages illustrates the motivation, hopes and ultimately the resourcefulness of those African Caribbean people who arrived here in the UK at that time. For example, in1952 Myrtle Lewars was in her early twenties when she decided to travel to Britain from Jamaica on the SS Columbia, a French vessel, which docked in Southampton. She is now retired after marrying and raising a family in London.

Myrtle Lewars left Jamaica to seek better employment opportunities as a seamstress as the pay was very poor in Jamaica. Like many others at the time she was encouraged to come to the UK by friends and family members who had arrived earlier. Myrtle was helped by new friends she met on the voyage to find accommodation with a Welsh family in South London. Initially unable to find employment as a seamstress, Myrtle took a job serving food in a local teashop which she disliked, but persevered with it, until eventually she was offered employment in a factory making blouses.

Like Myrtle Lewars the characters in Andrea Levy's book, "Small Island", tell vividly the type of experiences encountered by African Caribbean arrivals in the Britain as an ex-service man and a teacher, and their efforts to rise above the obstacles and disillusionment they faced in Britain, the 'mother country'.

It is generally accepted in the African Caribbean community that the many migrants in the period from 1948 to the early 1970s made use of the work opportunities to earn enough money then return to their homes in the Caribbean region, ideally with enough funds to sustain a better standard of living. For many of the first migrants the anecdotal belief is that the plan did not extend beyond this general goal.

However, for many of the later migrants who took the risk of seeking work in Britain in the 1960s, they held different objectives from their 1940s and 1950s counterparts. The economic conditions in the Caribbean region were still fragile, and jobs were difficult to find. Many of the later workers who travelled to Britain were older and had young families. For these African Caribbean travellers the ambition had two distinct features: seeking employment and accommodation that would be suitable for children; and saving enough money to allow them to send for their children, who in most cases were living with extended family members, such as grandparents, aunties and uncles, and cousins. Taking the risk of seeking work in Britain in the 1960s for many families was only possible because of the close and extended family support that these fathers and mothers could depend on in the Caribbean region.

What was life like in Britain for the early African Caribbean workers? We already know that Britain was struggling to recover from the destruction of homes, roads and factories, and it had a shortage of able bodied manpower. It is well documented that the British government's response to this situation was to invite people from the Caribbean region to contribute to the reconstruction and rebuilding effort. And indeed African Caribbean people responded. Many took the opportunities that existed in Britain to work, to earn, and to provide for their families. Sending money back to family members in the Caribbean islands was common practice as many "back home" were looking after the children of the adults working in Britain.

Records show that these later African Caribbean visitors quickly found work, but had greater difficulty finding suitable accommodations. The source of their accommodation issue was the general reluctance of British people to rent accommodations to African Caribbean people, who they did not know and regarded as foreigners. Many home owners would display signs in their windows that said, "no dogs, no Irish, no Blacks" making their feelings quite clear to all potential tenants.

The government and some charitable organisations provided temporary accommodations, but they were often over-crowded and were unsuitable for couples or families. Consequently, accommodation became the most urgent need for the African Caribbean workers in the post War decades.

The solution of choice for most was the partner system (popularly referred to in the African Caribbean community as the "pardner" system or the "susu" system, by a minority). This system was often used in Jamaica mainly by casual or non salaried workers in order to save their money and to access large sums for special situations.

The partner system was a method of saving money by groups of friends in which a trusted member would act as the bookkeeper and banker. Everyone would make regular contributions to the bookkeeper-cum-banker, and each week there would be a draw on the savings by one of the savers or partners. The sums accessed under the partner system would be quite large and this would enable the person making the draw to purchase expensive items that would be unaffordable from unpredictable weekly or monthly wages.

Furthermore, by choosing to save together many African Caribbean workers were able to raise large sums of money for down payments on their first homes and other important items that ordinarily would be out of their financial reach. This solution helped them to overcome two key difficulties. One was gaining access to reasonable accommodation that provided enough space for their families. The partner system also helped poor African Caribbean workers to get around the other annoying issue of the reluctance of managers in banks and building societies to lend money to them; which made it difficult for them to establish themselves in the British society. For a large number of African Caribbean workers the partner system was an important springboard for putting their ambitions and plans into action.

Despite these hurdles, the African Caribbean people were successful in Britain at solving the accommodation problem. The anecdotal belief was that they achieved a higher rate of home ownership than local white workers of the same income groups.

Other issues also became apparent to African Caribbean workers in the early decades after WW2. Many educated, qualified and experienced workers such as teachers were told by potential employers that their qualifications were not accepted in the UK. These claims by potential employers were actually incorrect as teachers' qualifications in the British Caribbean region were issued by British examination boards. Nevertheless, many were forced to accept work as unqualified teachers (which carried lower pay), or seek alternative employment that did not suit their training, education or skills.

Another issue facing African Caribbean workers in Britain was the unlawful behaviour of the police. The police services in the major urban areas such as London, Birmingham, Manchester and Cardiff began to target African Caribbean men as they went about their everyday affairs. The "sus law" was the excuse that the police services used to justify their behaviour, claiming that the chief reason for stopping and searching these men was that their alleged behaviour was deemed to be suspicious. These claims were made against African Caribbean men without any tangible evidence, except the word of a police officer. The unwarranted attacks on innocent African Caribbean men generated a great deal of unhappiness and caused the arrest of many, and inflicted criminal records wrongly on them.

A further upsetting matter emerged in the British school system. Large numbers of the children from African Caribbean families were systematically deprived of secondary education through the practice of teachers mis-categorising them as having special educational needs (SEN). This quickly led to these labelled children being removed from lessons and put in groups where they were offered inadequate learning support opportunities.

The situation for many children of African Caribbean workers worsened as headteachers' choice of punishment for African Caribbean teenagers was expulsion from school for alleged misbehaviour. It soon became clear that these expulsions peaked for these children in the age range 12 to 15, which coincided with the key years before public examinations such as the General Certificate of Education (GCE) or Certificate of Secondary Education (CSE).

There were two consequences of these issues for the children involved in these situations. The first, was where students were being expelled from schools they became vulnerable to being arrested by the police under the "sus law", if they wandered the streets. Secondly, these students' attention would be distracted from the preparation for public examinations. This meant that these children either did not take examinations or took the lower status CSE examinations, which were not valued by future employers.

African Caribbean families, who for decades had placed a high value on education in the Caribbean region, held a positive attitude to schools. Their starting point was to place their trust in the teachers in British schools, as much as they did in the Caribbean region. However, they soon discovered, to their cost, that this trust was misplaced when faced with the negative mindset of large numbers of teachers towards the children of African Caribbean origin who had begun entering the British education system.

African Caribbean people in Britain were also faced with the additional challenge of racially motivated attacks against them. These attacks were committed by mostly young white people on lone individuals who looked African Caribbean or African, and in the communities where they lived, such as the 1958 attacks in Notting Hill, London.

The Notting Hill Carnival was started in 1959 by an African Caribbean woman of action, Claudia Jones. This was as a direct response to these racially motivated riots, in an attempt to positively ease racial tensions in London.

The continued discrimination against African Caribbean people within Britain eventually prompted government legislation intended to outlaw racial discrimination. The first such legislation was the1965 Race Relations Act. This Act has been repealed and strengthened by subsequent Acts in 1968; 1976, which established the Commission for Racial Equality (CRE); and most recently the Equality Act of 2010.

There were other social issues to address but the ones already described were deeply upsetting and hurtful to African Caribbean families. The issues of accommodation, education, employment, unprovoked attacks and policing were challenges that the community tried to solve. This prompted many African Caribbean people to take action by participating in a range of community organisations that were set up to address these and other needs.

The African Caribbean workers that came to Britain were willing to take risks, they were ambitious, they were resilient, and they were enterprising. It is because of these personal qualities they were able to cope with these difficulties and challenges. They made significant progress towards overcoming them, while also establishing themselves in Britain. Some of their responses to these challenges and areas of contribution to British society are highlighted below:

Black majority churches
African Caribbean people set up and lead churches that responded to their spiritual and emotional needs once they discovered they were not welcome at most white run churches. In their own churches they provided fellowship and emotional relief from the hostility of the workplace, and the day to day social challenges. African Caribbean people became leaders of Black majority faith groups such as the New Testament Church of God (NTCG), Church of God of Prophecy (COGOP), Seventh-Day Adventist Church (SDAC) and others. Now there are hundreds of such churches across the UK.

Social housing network

African Caribbean people have played a significant role in the creation of a network for housing associations that provide social housing for poor and working class folks. This network of housing associations is known as BME National. It was founded in 2009 for continuing a service to poor African Caribbean people and other poor ethnic minority people that goes back to 1955 (the generation of the Windrush pioneers).

Supplementary schools

African Caribbean people set up and ran a nationwide network of voluntary schools on Saturdays to overcome the failure of state run schools in respect of their children. In these voluntary schools they empathised with the needs of African Caribbean children and worked to plug many of the gaps that the state schools allowed to develop. Dr Keith Davidson and Dr June Alexis have described this situation fully in their book, "Education, a pathway to success for black children", published in 2012. There are also networks of mentoring organisations devoted to motivating and supporting talented young people of African Caribbean origin to develop their full potential. Chief amongst them are Excell3 based in Wolverhampton, and ACES Youth Project based in London.

Credit unions & partner systems

African Caribbean people set up and ran credit unions and partner systems in urban areas of Britain that provided access to loans that could not be obtained from banks and building societies. In so doing they were able to establish themselves in their own homes, start small businesses, and acquire essential items for their families.

Self help organisations

African Caribbean people set up and ran hundreds of clubs and organisations in major urban centres for meeting their social needs in areas not met by the white British community. Some familiar names include the many Caribbean Associations in parts of Greater London, Manchester and Birmingham.

Others organisations included the Family Tree Association that was founded in North London by Ancel Lewars and friends. This association organised dinner dances, outings for families and friends within the UK, and trips abroad for over twenty years from the 1960s, at a time when African Caribbean families tended to stay close to their homes in the large urban areas.

There was the Parents Association for Black Educational Advance that was founded in the 1970s in North West London by Ambrozine Neil and a group of parents. This association was able to offer support to local parents who needed help to deal with the many cases of exclusion of their children from schools.

Networks for professionals

African Caribbean people set up and ran groups that enabled their experts and professionals to network with each other, championed the cause for equity of treatment and access to opportunities.

These included groups such as the Society of Black Lawyers, founded in 1969; the Black Training and Enterprise Group founded in 1991; the Black Police Association founded in 1994; the Network for Black Professionals, founded in 1995; and many others.

Business entrepreneurs

African Caribbean people who became entrepreneurs included Tony Wade director of Dyke & Dryden Ltd that created the UK's hair care industry for African Caribbean people at a time when banks were unwilling to support enterprise in the community. Furthermore, retail outlets were not inclined to stock products for just African Caribbean consumers.

Others entrepreneurs included Joy Nichols, founder of Nichols Employment Agency (NEA); Leroy Reid, founder of Leroy Reid & Co, accountancy services; Michael Webster and Dawn Dixon, founders of Webster Dixon Solicitors; Val McCalla, founder of The Voice Newspaper that specialised in news for the African Caribbean community in Britain; Piers Linney, founder of Outsourcery, a cloud technology IT service provider; John La Rose, founder of New Beacon Books that published the works of African Caribbean writers; and Keith Valentine Graham Bilal Musa (aka Levi Roots), the creator and supplier of Reggae Reggae Sauce. He is also an author and musician.

In addition, there are large numbers of others who became micro-entrepreneurs in a range of sectors such as black cab taxi-drivers, training consultants; and thousands of others who founded hair salons and barber shops in cities and large towns in Britain.

Private sector

African Caribbean workers have launched and established themselves in employment in most parts of the private sector such as accountancy;

the law (as solicitors and barristers) with Courtney Griffiths being one of many outstanding barristers.

In banking and finance Trevor Williams, chief economist, at Lloyds Bank is one of many in this area. In broadcast media there are well known presenters such as Sir Trevor McDonald (at ITV), Clive Myrie and Moira Stewart (at the BBC), and Juliette Foster (at Sky TV and the BBC). In print media there are Darcus Howe and many African Caribbean journalists working at the GV Media Group, the publishers of The Voice and Gleaner newspapers, and on the broadsheets newspapers such as Joseph Harker, at The Guardian.

There are many African Caribbean people in the property sector both as staff in estate agents, and as property owners and landlords. In the IT and communication sector there are large numbers of African Caribbean people engaged as engineers and IT experts. In reality, African Caribbean people in Britain are employed in virtually all areas of the private sectors.

Local decision making
Large numbers of African Caribbean people became involved in the local democratic decision making processes in Britain by becoming branch officers and elected councillors through the established political parties such as Labour, Conservatives and Liberal Democrats in both urban and rural areas.

National decision making
African Caribbean people became elected MPs via national political parties and served in the House of Commons. In 1987 two African Caribbean members of the Labour Party became MPs. They were Diane Abbott and Bernie Grant. They were followed by others such as David Lammy. African Caribbean people also served in the House of Lords, they include Lord Herman Ouseley, Lord Bill Morris, Baroness Valerie Amos, and Baroness Patricia Scotland.

Trade union movement
African Caribbean people joined the trade unions and rose to leadership positions. For example, in 1991 Bill Morris became general secretary of the TGWU (Transport & General Workers Union), becoming the first African Caribbean person to lead a national trade union in Britain. He later he became Lord Bill Morris and entered the House of Lords. Many African Caribbean people are prominent in other trade unions such as the National Union of Teachers (NUT).

Public sector
Health, transportation, postal service, education and social housing are significant parts of the public sector, and African Caribbean people employed in them have also became experts and leaders in these areas. Workers from African Caribbean origin are to be found at all levels of the public sector.

African Caribbean people also became civil servants, and served in the police, fire and armed services. In the education field African Caribbean people became experts and leaders in all stages of this service. They are employed in the different sectors of education such as primary, secondary, further education and higher education in universities.

Entertainment - sport
African Caribbean young people started marking their mark in county cricket but soon took a keen interest in football (Garth Crooks, Brendan Batson, Mark Chamberlain, Vince Hilaire and many others) and athletics (Denise Lewis, Jessica Ennis, Linford Christie, Colin Jackson, Dwain Chambers and many others) to be more rewarding and lucrative; in addition, they have entered other high profile sports such as Formula One (F1) motor racing (Lewis Hamilton).

Entertainment - music and drama
African Caribbean people founded bands and became entertainers. Some examples include Matumbi, a reggae band (founded in 1971); Soul 2 Soul (founded in 1982 by Trevor Beresford Romeo aka Jazzy B); Kenny Lynch and Norman Beaton (actors), Lenny Henry (comedian & actor), Colin Salmon (actor & musician), Sharon Duncan-Brewster and Naomie Harris (actresses), and Adrian Lester (actor) are a selection.

In the early years of the 21st Century, English speakers of African Caribbean origins have been in Britain for almost 65 years. The majority of the African Caribbean workers, who arrived in the decade from 1948, have retired and their children are in the later years of their working lives. Their grand children are now among the young people in this community, all were born in Britain, which makes them fully British of African Caribbean background.

At the beginning of the 21st century, the children and grandchildren of African Caribbean workers are undoubtedly British citizens, and large numbers can be seen in all aspects of life in British society. African Caribbean engagement in a small number of fields of employment such as teaching, nursing, public transportation and semi-skilled jobs has increased to virtually all sectors of employment. Today, African Caribbean people are also engaged in sectors such as local government, civil service, social care, finance, legal, manufacturing, engineering, academia and the voluntary sector. Today British people of African Caribbean origin have created a community which has many distinct and positive features such as the ones described below.

African Caribbean middle class

The African Caribbean community contains a class of highly educated people, who are professionals in many fields. They are at the core of the middle class which has steadily grown since the middle of the 20th Century.

African Caribbean entrepreneurs and high earners

The African Caribbean community contains a class of people who have generated millions through business ownership such as Piers Linney, the founder of Outsourcery, an IT service provider; Leroy Reid, the founder of Leroy Reid & Co, accountancy; Joy Nichols, the founder of Nichols Employment Agency; and through sporting accomplishments by the likes of Rio Ferdinand, Theo Walcott, Alex Oxlade-Chamberlain, Lewis Hamilton, Jessica Ennis, Denise Lewis, Colin Jackson, Garth Crooks and many others.

African Caribbean political leaders

The African Caribbean community contains a class of people who have continued the breakthrough into national political leadership that was pioneered by Lord Laurie Constantine (1950s) and Lord David Pitt (1960s). The current group of political leaders include Lord Herman Ouseley, Baroness Valerie Amos, Baroness Patricia Scotland, Diane Abbott, MP and David Lammy MP.

African Caribbean experts

The African Caribbean community contains a class of professionals who are experts in their fields such as Sir William Atkinson, a super headteacher, Dr Keith Davidson, headteacher and author; Dr June Alexis, headteacher and author; Dr Jasmine Rhamie, university senior lecturer & author; Dr Donald Palmer, senior lecturer in immunology, Royal Veterinary College; Dr Roxanne Ferdinand, haematology specialist; Robin Walker, historian and black studies expert; Courtney Griffiths, QC (a barrister) and there are many others.

African Caribbean networks

The African Caribbean community contains a number of networking groups that enables its professionals to regularly interact with each other and with professionals from other communities and backgrounds. These include the Black Lawyers Society, the Black Police Association, the Network for Black Professionals; and Reach Society, a network of professional Black men (of African Caribbean and African origins).

What is quite clear is that at the start of the 21st Century the African Caribbean community in Britain is in a quite different position than it was in the first decade after 1948. It is more robust, it is now a community that fully understands the systems, institutions and the culture in Britain. It has educated experts; a growing middle class; a distinct wealthy class; a range of capabilities; and many African Caribbean people involved in the voluntary sector, trade union movement and the major political parties.

Overall, the British people of African Caribbean origin have risen to the challenges they faced on arrival back in 1948, and they have made use of the many new opportunities in Britain to develop themselves and their families. After almost 65 years the British people of African Caribbean origin are more mature and robust to deal with challenges and make full use of their potential and the opportunities that are available. How they make use of their many capabilities and accumulated knowledge will further shape their destiny in Britain.

Chapter 5

The 21st Century, facing the future with confidence
(2013 to 2099, roughly 86 years, or the next 3.5 generations)

In the previous chapter we tried to highlight the many areas of participation and achievement for British people of African Caribbean origin in their first 65 years in Britain. In this chapter we shall be taking a look ahead. What can we foresee across the next three to four generations, over a period of almost 90 years, to the end of the 21st Century?

But first, it is worth recording that the changes that took place in the past for African Caribbean people came about because of the efforts of men and women of action from their community and in part from the prevailing climate at the time. During the wilderness years we have shown that a good many African men and women of action resisted the abusive culture of the time. They played their part in helping to bring about the ending of an era of systematic abuse.

During the era of growth and development we have shown that a good many African Caribbean men and women of action inspired and led the formation of groups and organisations that championed the need for social and political change. They pressured the establishment to be more just and more inclusive. In addition, at the family level they worked to increase the capability of children who have achieved success in many facets of life beyond being simple labourers on the land.

During the era of new opportunities and new challenges in Britain we have shown that African Caribbean men and women of action took great risks in travelling overseas in pursuit of work and opportunities that were not on offer in the Caribbean region. And once again, at the family level they worked to increase the capability of their children who have achieved success in a wide range of sectors in Britain. Furthermore, African Caribbean people have built and led institutions that have lasted for over fifty years, and they continue to build new institutions in response to needs that have not been fully satisfied.

There is no doubt that relative to their starting point, as newly freed people in 1834, the foregoing achievements and contributions have been significant. The African Caribbean men and women of action have made a difference to generations of their descendants.

Records tell us that many African Caribbean people also went in search of opportunity in Canada and the USA. However, our focus in this publication is on the ones who chose to travel to and make their way in Britain. So what do we foresee for the British people of African Caribbean origin across the next three or four generations, to the end of the 21st Century?

It is our belief that by taking stock of where we are today and by identifying the issues and obstacles that lie ahead, it should be possible for our community to chart its way ahead. Like the Windrush pioneers, today's African Caribbean people will need to adapt and apply their creativity in order to continue the process for shaping their future.

Thus, in keeping with this heritage of assessing the challenges before us, we present a brief backdrop to the issues facing the British African Caribbean community for the 21st century. As a community we need to be fully aware of this, using certain key economic, social and educational indicators. The metrics below, taken from the National Labour Force Survey 2007 and 2008, suggest a number of concerns.

Firstly, current employment and education status statistics show that approximately 30% to 45% of Black young people (from both African and African Caribbean origins) between the ages of 16 to 24 are in the NEET category (i.e. not in employment, education or training).

Secondly, employment figures for the last decade show that the employment level for the general population remains at roughly 75%, in contrast the employment level for Black and minority ethnic (BME) workers has been hovering around the 60% mark. This means that consistently there has been a 15% employment gap between BME workers and the general population.

Thirdly, the employment problem facing the British African Caribbean community becomes more acute for the younger age group, as the employment rate for British African Caribbean people, between 16 and 29, is approximately 45%. In other words, more than half of this age group cannot be found participating in the workplace.

Fourthly, on the pay and remuneration front, Black male graduates (from both African and African Caribbean origins) earn 24% less than White British male graduates. This could partly be attributable to differences in the type of university attended (whether they were high value institutions like the 24 universities in the Russell Group or not). However, this is part of an overall picture of unequal pay and remuneration for this class of workers.

Fifthly, with respect to professional occupations and this in some way is linked to the fourth point above, only one in ten (10%) men of African and African Caribbean origin are employed in professional jobs. This is half the rate for all men (which 2 in 10). In contrast, men from Chinese and Indian backgrounds are nearly twice as likely (around 4 in 10) as White British men to be in professional jobs.

Finally, in the area of national secondary education achievement, the trend over the last five years has been one of significant increase in achievement from around 35% rising to roughly 50% of British children of African Caribbean origin obtaining the benchmark 5 A*- C, GCSE examination results, including English and mathematics. This shows that the African Caribbean community has continued to meet the challenge for improving the achievement of it children. However, the educational underachievement of roughly half of British children of African Caribbean origin should continue to be a major concern for the community in the 21st century.

And so with this concise economic, social and education profiling, here are some of the issues we feel that British people of African Caribbean origin need to consider and address as we look ahead:

Community and cultural esteem – there is a need for the provision of more high quality information about the on going contributions of British people of African Caribbean origin, as this will help to raise and maintain the cultural and ethnic esteem within generations of our young people.

Leadership contribution – there is a need for the creation of sustainable approaches for protecting and supporting those British people of African Caribbean origin who have been less successful in this community.

Education challenges – there is a need for the community to design and control systems that ensure consistent high quality education for its children, so that their innate talents are not squandered or under-developed in a state education system that has many fault lines; and falls well short of being fully fit for purpose.

Financial challenges – there is a need for greater access to and control of sources of sustainable employment and wealth generation for the benefit of the African Caribbean community, and the wider community.

Housing challenge – there is a need for a fresh approach for reducing the over-reliance on social housing by a sizeable segment of the African Caribbean community and replacing it with a higher level of home ownership.

Social challenges – there is a need for systems that ensure the development of robust personal qualities in all of our young people, so that they will be inoculated from the more destructive components of life in the wider British community.

Criminal justice system (CJS) and care system challenges – there is a need for work on strategies designed to keep unsupported African Caribbean young people from falling prey to the twin pitfalls of the care system and the CJS; and to help them to develop viable life-skills for successfully navigating adult life.

Health challenges – there is a need for work on strategies for raising the understanding of how to improve the lifestyle choices and develop better knowledge of how to maintain robust physical and mental health.

Political challenges – there is a need for sustained access to political structures to influence important decisions that affect the quality of life in the African Caribbean community, and the wider British community.

This list of nine issues to address is neither exhaustive nor exclusive to the African Caribbean community. However, it is our belief that with the African Caribbean community taking a closer interest in these areas, it will influence the life chances and the destiny of large numbers in its community, especially those who have suffered serious misfortune, and have not been as successful in making good enough or adequate provision for themselves and their families.

Perhaps the best way of capturing these important future challenges for the African Caribbean community is to urge it to find a systematic way of showing compassion to those who need help to become viable and robust; such that they too will be able to contribute more to their families, the African Caribbean community, and the wider community in Britain.

Across the UK there is clear evidence of compassionate work in the African Caribbean community, but in order to realise the synergy that is needed to help a greater number of its people, the dots need to be connected.

Therefore, it is our belief that this should be the priority for the 21st Century. By raising the awareness of the young British people of African Caribbean origin to fully understand the achievements of their parents and grand parents, to fully understand who they are, and what they are capable of achieving. They should come to understand this priority for their community. It is our belief that by undertaking this challenge, and becoming a man or woman of action, the growth and development of British people of African Caribbean origin would continue in the 21st century.

It is our belief that the British people of African Caribbean origin have a full range of capabilities at their disposal to engage and deal effectively with the aforementioned issues. In so doing they will continue the process that their forefathers started in 1834, for taking ever more responsibility for the people in their community, and continue the effort to shape their unique destiny.

African Caribbean timeline from 1834 to 1950s

Appendix 1 – African Caribbean timeline of civil and political rights

- **1834** Emancipation of enslaved African Caribbean people (in all British colonies).

- **1835** First free African Caribbean men (5) elected to Jamaican Assembly.

- **1838** End of apprenticeship scheme (in virtually all British colonies).

- **1865** Direct rule by Britain imposed on Jamaica (Crown Colony) triggered by the hanging of Paul Bogle an African Caribbean Baptist deacon and campaigner for social improvements for the poor.

- **1870s** British Guyana, beginnings of demands for political rights by African Caribbean population.

- **1876** Barbados protests against restrictions on freedom of African Caribbean people, against the lack of voting rights and against bad living conditions on plantations.

- **1879** Jamaica: Lady Musgrave Women's Self Help Society founded to develop local industries and provide employment to poor craftswomen.

- **1897** Trinidad Workingmen's Association formed, although trade unions were not legal.

- **1898** Jamaica: Peoples Convention established by Robert Love to promote the collective interests of African Caribbean people. Love advocated women's rights in general, education of African Caribbean women and universal adult suffrage.

- **1900** London, UK: The first Pan-African conference held; it was organised by Henry S. Williams from Trinidad. He advocated women's rights in general and the education of African Caribbean women.

- **1901** Trinidad: Henry. S. Williams founded the Pan African Association.

- **1901** Peoples Convention Conference - Catherine McKenzie spoke on the subject of women's rights.

- **1901** Trinidad Home Industries and Women's Self-Help Association founded by women concerned with providing earning opportunities for women.

- **1909** Jamaica: National Club formed by Robert Love; it was the first nationalist organisation on the island.

- **1914 -1918** World War 1: African Caribbean people fought with Britain.

- **1914** Jamaica: Marcus Garvey and Amy Ashwood Garvey established the United Negro Improvement Association (UNIA). Amy A. Garvey founded the ladies division. UNIA was one of the few early nationalist organizations which always had positions for women in its executive.

- **1916-1919** Series of strikes across the Caribbean: In St Lucia, Grenada, Barbados, Antigua, Trinidad, Jamaica and British Guyana. Strikes inspired by local grievances, by anger at the racist treatment of African Caribbean soldiers during and after World War 1 (WW1), and by the example of the 1917 Russian revolution.

- **1918** British West Indian Regiment: Mutiny at Taranto by African Caribbean soldiers over lower pay than for white soldiers. Following the mutiny, a group of 60 non-commissioned officers met to discuss African Caribbean rights, self-determination and closer union in the West Indies. They formed the Caribbean League and decided to hold a general strike for higher wages on their return to the West Indies.

- **1918** London: Society of Peoples of African Origin formed by Rev. F.E.M. Hercules (a Trinidadian) with a group of African Caribbean businessmen and students.

- **1918** Jamaica: Women's Social Service Club (WSSC) was founded.

- **1921** Trinidad: Audrey Jeffers founded the Coterie of Social Workers; it was aimed at improving the status of middle class African Caribbean women; at the time social work was the preserve of middle class white women.

- **1924** Trinidad: Deputation of women to the Governor of Trinidad to discuss votes for women.

- **1928** Jamaica: Marcus Garvey founded the Peoples Political Party. His work inspired a new sense of racial self-respect. He laid a foundation that inspired the organised movement for nationalism in the Caribbean that commenced in the late 1930s.

- **1929** Jamaica: Una Marson became editor of Jamaica's first women's publication, The Cosmopolitan. It was the official publication of the Jamaica Stenographers Association and it called for increased employment opportunities for working-class women.

- **1936** Trinidad: The Coterie of Social Workers hosted the first conference of women social workers in the British Caribbean; and it formed the Association of Women Workers.

- **1936** Trinidad: Audrey Jeffers was the first woman elected to the Port of Spain City Council.

- **1936** Trinidad: Married women teachers were barred from employment.

- **1937** Jamaica: Women's Liberal Club formed.

- **1933** Across the Caribbean: Labour unrest, strikes and protests had been occurring in response to extensive unemployment and under-employment, low wages, the high cost of everyday essential goods and the racist attitudes of colonial administrators and employers.

  While trade unions had been legalised in some countries in the Caribbean region, there were no collective bargaining mechanisms to settle industrial disputes. Despite the use of armed police and soldiers and many deaths of those who challenged the power of the employers and the government of the colonies, the unrest continued and culminated in a general strike in Trinidad in 1937. There were strikes across Jamaica for many weeks in the same year and thirty disputes involving over 12,000 workers in British Guyana in 1938.

- **1938** After the uprisings wages increased, unions were made lawful in all Caribbean countries, the African Caribbean middle class gained more access to civil service jobs and the professions; and they formed political parties.

- **1938** Jamaica: The Bustamante Industrial Trades Union (BITU) founded by Alexander Bustamante. He also founded the Jamaica Labour Party, JLP.

- **1938** Jamaica: The People's National Party (PNP) founded by Norman Manley.

- **1938** Following the labour unrest across the Caribbean region, a Royal Commission (the Moyne Commission) was set up to investigate social and economic conditions in British-ruled Caribbean.

- **1939 -1945** World War 2: African Caribbean men and women joined the British forces.

- **1939** Trinidad: Women were barred from night work in factories.

- **1940** Moyne Commission published its recommendations, but the full report was not published until 1945 for fear of further civil unrest. The Commission recommended that there should be just male bread winners, stable monogamy and a campaign against promiscuity, voluntary social work for middle class women, as well as opportunities in the professions and civil service. Education in domestic science was advocated for working class girls. It showed distinct bias towards middle class women and said nothing about equal pay.

- **1942** Jamaica Youth Movement formed.

- **1944** Jamaican Federation of Women (JFW) founded by the wife of the Colonial Governor. It was modelled on the British Women's Institutes. The aims of the JFW were consistent with the Royal Commission report. The JFW also opposed universal adult suffrage and wanted literacy qualification for adults.

- **1946** Trinidad: Audrey Jeffers appointed to the Legislative Council of Trinidad by the Governor. As a member of the Franchise Committee she voted against immediate Universal Adult Suffrage.

- **1948** Jamaica Federation of Women had 30,000 members after just 4 years.

- **1952** Jamaica: National Workers Union (NWU) founded by Norman Manley and others. The NWU became an affiliate of the Peoples National Party (PNP) which he founded.

- **1956** Audrey Jeffers initiated a Caribbean Women's Conference, aimed at forming a Caribbean Women's Association (CWA). One of the aims of the CWA was to encourage women's active participation in all aspects of social, economic and political life in the Caribbean and to work for the removal of the remaining restrictions on the legal, economic and social rights of women.

Appendix 2 – African Caribbean timeline of adult suffrage (voting right)

(1918 In Britain all men aged 21 and women aged 30 meeting property qualifications gained the right to vote; and 10 years later, in 1928, all women over 21 gained the right to vote, removing the property qualification).

- **1935-1936** Women in Trinidad got the vote in local elections.

- **1944** Adult suffrage and a degree of self-government gained; and Sex Disqualification (Removal) Act introduced in Jamaica.

- **1946** Universal adult suffrage in Trinidad.

- **1950** Universal adult suffrage in Barbados.

- **1951** Women got same voting rights as men in St Vincent.

- **1951** Universal Adult Suffrage in Dominica.

- **1953** Women got the vote in British Guiana (renamed Guyana at independence).

Appendix 3 – African Caribbean timeline, Independence from Britain

- **1957** Self-government in Jamaica.

- **1962** Jamaica and Trinidad & Tobago gained independence from Britain.

- **1966** Barbados and British Guiana gained independence from Britain. Once independence came British Guiana changed its name to Guyana.

- **1978** Dominica gained independence from Britain.

- **1979** Saint Vincent and the Grenadines gained independence from Britain.

We note with thanks the sources of the photographs used in this publication:

- **Adrian Lester (actor in Hustle, BBC series)** – photo from Wikipedia;
- **Andrea Levy (prize winning author)** – photo from British Council website;
- **Baroness Valerie Amos** (erstwhile chair, Equal Opportunities Commission & Labour Party minister) – photo from Wikipedia;
- **Colin Jackson** (world record 110m hurdler) – photo from BBC website;
- **Courtney Pine** (pioneering musicians & performers) - photo from Wikipedia;
- **David Lammy, MP** - photo from Wikipedia;
- **Diane Abbott** (first Black British female MP) – photo from local press, Tottenham;
- **Dame Jocelyn Barrow** (community champion for social change) – photo from National Portrait Gallery website;
- **Dr Harold Moody** (medical doctor & founder of the League of Coloured People, 1931) from 100 Great Black Britons website;
- **Dr Alison Wint** (medical doctor & daughter of Dr Arthur Wint, 1948 Olympic 400m gold medallist – a first by an African Caribbean person);
- **Dr Keith Davidson** (headteacher & director of education) –photo from KAD Publications website;
- **Dr Donald Palmer** (scientist & senior lecturer, University of London) – photo from Reach Society website;
- **Garth Crooks** (premier league footballer) – photo from Mail Online;
- **Jazzy B** (careers news presenter) - photo from100 Great Black Britons website;
- **Jessica Ennis** (2012 heptathlon Olympic champion) – photo from Mirror Online;

- **John Barnes** (premier league footballer) – photo from Wikipedia;
- **Juliette Foster** (news presenter Sky News & BBC) – photo from Wikipedia.
- **Leroy Reid** (founder of Leroy Reid & Co, accountancy firm);
- **Lord Bill Morris** (former leader of the Transport & General Worker's Union from 1991) photo from Wikipedia;
- **Lord Herman Ouseley** (former chairman of the Commission for Racial Equality) – photo from100 Great Black Britons website;
- **Linford Christie** (sprinter & 100m Olympic Champion) - photo from100 Great Black Britons website;
- **Louis Smith** (Gymnast, 2012 Olympic silver medallist) – photo from Wikipedia;
- **Moira Stewart** (careers news presenter) – photo from The Guardian Online;
- **Naomie Harris** (actress featured in Skyfall, 007 movie) - photo from Wikipedia;
- **Robin Walker** (teacher, historian, author & black studies expert) – photo from Robin Walker's website;
- **Sir Trevor McDonald** (careers news presenter) - photo from100 Great Black Britons website;
- **Theo Walcott** (premier league footballer) - photo from Wikipedia;
- **Tony Wade** (entrepreneur & director of Dyke & Dryden) – photo from Wikipedia
- **Val McCalla** (founder of The Voice newspaper, 1982) – from 100 Great Black Britons website;
- **Zadie Smith** (prize winning author) - photo from Wikipedia.

Adrian Lester, actor

Andrea Levy

Baroness Patricia Scotland

Baroness Valerie Amos

Colin Jackson

Courtney Pine

Dame Jocelyn Barrow

David Lammy, MP

Diane Abbott, MP

Dr Donald Palmer

Dr Harold Moody

Dr Keith Davidson

Garth Crooks

Jazzie B

Jessica Ennis

John Barnes

Juliette Foster

Linford Christie

Lord Bill Morris

Lord Herman Ouseley

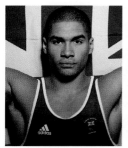

Louis Smith

Moira Stewart

Naomie Harris

Robin Walker

Sir Trevor McDonald

Theo Walcott

Tony Wade

Val McCalla

Zadie Smith

Bibliography

Below are sources that were found to be useful in the preparation of this publication:

- **Chapter 1: Who do you think you are?**
  100 Great Black Britons; http://www.100greatblackbritons.com
  The abbreviated history of Barbados; www.Barbados.org/history
  Tony Wade, "How they made a million", published by Hansib Publication, 2001.
  Tony Wade, "The adventures of an economic migrant", Ian Randle Publishers, 2007
  Valerie Wint, "The longer run", published by Ian Randle Publishers, 2012

- **Chapter 2: The Wilderness Years**
  Higham, B. W. 1984. Slave populations of the British Caribbean, 1807-1834. Baltimore: Johns Hopkins University Press.
  Veront Satchell, Africana.com, 1999; www.hartford-hwp.com/archives

- **Chapter 3: The age of growth and development**
  Engerman, Stanley L. 1984. Economic change and contract labor in the British Caribbean:
  The end of slavery and the adjustment to emancipation, Explorations in Economic History 21: 133-50.
  P. Emmer, '"A Spirit of Independence" or Lack of Education for the Market? Freedman and Asian Indentured Labourers in the Post-Emancipation Caribbean, 1834–1917', in After Slavery. Emancipation and its Discontents, ed. H. Temperly (London, 2000), pp 150–168.
  Pieter C. Emmer, 'Scholarship or Solidarity? The Post-Emancipation Era in the Caribbean Reconsidered', New West Indian Guide, 69.3 (1995), 277–90;
  Michael J. Craton, 'Response to Pieter C. Emmer's "Reconsideration"', New West India Guide, 69.3 (1995), 291–7.
  Sandra W. Meditz and Dennis M. Hanratty, editors. Caribbean Islands: A Country Study. Washington: GPO for the Library of Congress, 1987.

- **Chapter 4: The age of new opportunities and new challenges**
  Andrea Levy, "Small Island", published by Headline book Publishing, 2004
  Keith Davidson & June Alexis, "Education, A pathway to success for black children, published by KAD Publishing, 2012
  Mike Phillips & Trevor Phillips, "Windrush, the irresistible rise of multi-racial Britain", publisher Harper Collins Publishers, 1998

- **Chapter 5: The 21st Century, facing the future with confidence**
  Office for National Statistics; National Labour Force Survey 2007 & 2008.